BREAKING THE CHAINS

Teaching Your Kids the Money Lessons You Weren't Taught

JACQUELINE B SCHAFFER & DESMOND RUCKER II

Thank You	4
Who Taught Me About Money	7
Hustle 101	8
Preparing for College	11
Pregnant in College	12
Where Does Money Come From	16
Production of Money	16
Career Choice	19
Earning Money	24
What is Money Management?	31
Bills	31
Saving	32
Investing	33
Fun	34
Debt	35
Value of Money	41
Break it Down	43
Investing	45
Saving	46
Saving Money & Setting Goals	49
Saving Style	49
529 Plans	53
Buying a Car	56
Take the Fear out of Finance	58
Being a Good Example	58
Financial Activities	59
Building Your Child's Credit	62
Parts of a Credit Score	64
Banking for Kids	68
Bank Accounts	68
Investing	68

Kidpreneurs	71
Why Does This Matter?	**75**
Financial Terms	**78**
Savings Chart	**82**
Goal Worksheet	**83**
Savings Passbook	**84**
Flashcards on Next Page	**85**
Flashcards	**86**

Thank You

I first want to thank you as the reader, for making this small investment into my brand, that will be a huge investment into your future. Writing this book was extremely important to me because my purpose in life is to help people reach their goals, particularly parents. Our babies are the future of the world and raising them correctly will either destroy the world as we know it or make it flourish. As an auntie, big cousin, big sister and now mom of two, I have continuously done all I can to prepare the next generation with tutoring and mentoring.

In this book I share the financial lessons that I have learned and taught to the youth in my life over the past few years. This book was written for parents, aunties/uncles, godmoms/dads, teachers and community leaders who would like to make sure they are educated on finances so that they can share these lessons with the children in their life. I have helped many clients in the past four years fix their budgets and their credit scores, so that they can reach their financial goals. So many parents have had their children in mind when building these plans, either wanting to build an empire for the child to profit off of later or starting a business for the child.

When I was eighteen years old I had my first son and I was completely clueless about how I would take care of him. I worked three jobs, I finished college and I have always made my decisions based off of his best interest. As I gained more knowledge about money, I have learned to save, invest and prepare him for financial success.

I also want to thank my grandmother Jacqueline Y, my aunt Cindy and my sister Ebony, for always being great examples of how to make it happen for your kids. This project would not have been released without their encouragement, lessons and mistakes. It's hard work raising kids, but I salute them for always making a way!

I of course saved the best for last. I want to thank Creation for giving me the vision and ensuring that I was able to complete this project. I procrastinated for months, just as I did with book one. Though I'm still working through issues of self-doubt, I knew that I wanted to get this information out before I went on maternity leave. So even while my house was being renovated from a tree crash and I was exhausted from growing a baby, I pulled all-nighters from the bed of my AirBNB to make this thing happen! I hope the information presented in this book helps you become more efficient with your money and equips you to teach your children to do the same.

The goal of this book is to teach you how to manage your finances appropriately, so that your children don't fall as slaves to the system. Many of us have had (or currently have) jobs that we hate and we beat ourselves up everyday knowing that we have to go, to make ends meet. I want to teach my sons to be self-sufficient on all levels, especially when it comes to money. My goal is to teach you how to make your money work for you, so that you can retire early, enjoy your life and teach your kids how to do the same. I feel blessed to be able to share my life experiences, to help people avoid some of the issues I faced. Open your mind and turn the page, it's time to break the chains!

Who Taught Me About Money

I decided to write this book to help other parents who grew up without financial knowledge, but who are dedicated to teaching their kids the correct way to manage money. If you grew up without knowledge on credit, income streams, stocks and interest; this book is for you. I grew up without being taught about any of these topics, but I bumped my head young and learned the lessons that matter to start building my financial empire. This book will share these lessons with you so that you can learn without hurting your credit or facing bankruptcy like I have. I hope that you share these lessons with the children in your life so that they too can learn from my mistakes and begin a positive financial journey.

Many of my money lessons were self-taught. So that means I had no advice on what were good rules to follow when it came to spending, saving or investing. The one thing I was taught was hustle. I was always encouraged to make my own money, even at a young age. This lesson was unconsciously taught to me by my grandma and the many entrepreneurs in my family. While some of them own brick and mortar businesses, others thrive in real estate. Then there are those who are silent about their income streams, I just know that they don't work for anybody else. I desired to be like them, to control my life and make my own money. So I followed their footsteps and I started my first business when I was only eight years old. Let me take you down memory lane and share my first money lessons with you.

Hustle 101

My first business was selling candy to my third-grade classmates. I only had one competitor, so I felt great about my ability to profit. Every day after school I would go to the local corner store and I would stock up on the most popular candy. Typically, I left the store with a bag of easy to open and eat candy. Sour Punch bites were always a top seller and I always was confident that those would be sold out before lunch. While I easily had the upper-hand on the competition by offering the best prices and best variety, I learned an early lesson about business that made my profits soar. If I could cut the purchase price of my candy, I could increase my profit margin. I also would have the ability to reduce my price if I wanted to.

The owner of the local corner store became a close family friend and when he discovered I was selling candy at school, he offered to take me to the wholesale store. I was able to drastically cut my price per unit. Cutting my price to attract more customers would be a good idea, but I thought of something better. It was at eight years old that I realized the power of a great bundle deal. Instead of only selling my candy for five cents a piece, I began to offer six pieces for a quarter. It was a hit and my business was a success for nearly two years. But, then the school discovered what we were doing and came down hard with new rules to stop us from selling candy. To avoid suspension, I left the candy hustle and started my second business.

My second hustle was making beaded jewelry. I went to the craft store to get clasps, good quality string and jewelry glue, I already had a ton of beads in different varieties. I spent about twenty dollars and went right to work creating pieces when I got home. I made a variety of matching sets and created a price list. I used a Mary Kay carrying case to carry and showcase my finished pieces. Once I had everything ready, I set up in front of our apartment building. It was a great location for two reasons, it was on the same corner as a bus stop and there was a commercial building across the street. In this business I learned two important business lessons, location is important, but ensuring that I make a healthy profit is just as important. I didn't charge enough for my bracelets and necklaces, so almost all of the money I made had to go right back into the business to make more pieces. I ended up moving on from this hustle and started babysitting family members and local neighborhood kids. That's when I learned that the service industry had a better profit margin than the product industry, due to the lack of overhead.

Outside of my independent sources of income, there was also a short period of time when I also received an allowance. My grandma gave me twenty-five dollars a month, as long as I did my chores. Being that it was just me and my grandmother it didn't take much to keep the house clean, so chores were never the problem. The issue was that I knew nothing about money. I didn't think about saving or investing or anything outside of spending. The money was usually gone in a week or two, spent on nothing but snacks from the local corner store. As much as I wish my grandma would have taught me more about money, I know that she didn't have the financial knowledge or she would have shared it with me. We lived in low income housing and my grandma did an extremely great job stretching her limited budget to always ensure the bills were paid, the kitchen was stocked and I kept clean clothes on my back.

By the time I was sixteen I decided it was time to get a real job. I would soon be a senior in high school and I knew that I had upcoming expenses if I wanted to apply for college. My first job was at Steak & Shake and I immediately started to take responsibility for my needs, to alleviate the burden on my grandma. So that meant my toiletries, my clothes, my shoes, all began to be purchased out of my personal income. This is when I first started budgeting. I would estimate how much my check would be based on my scheduled hours and after subtracting taxes. I would then determine what my priorities were and start developing my budget. I would ensure that the first line item was always my needs, such as soap, razors, pads and my cell phone bill. I would then divide the remaining amount into savings and fun. If I knew a movie I wanted to see was coming out or that a friend was having a party, I would plan for it in advance. Back then I didn't have a set percentage for my savings, but I was sure to always put something away.

Preparing for College

Senior year arrived and I was financially ready. I worked an internship throughout the summer to save additional cash and to ensure that everything went as planned. Though my family pitched in to handle as much as they could, quite a few expenses still came out of my pocket. Including my prom dress, my Cedar Point ticket for our senior celebration and most of my dorm essentials. I walked into college with $900 in my pocket and an awesome resume. I landed my first work study job before the second week of class. It was a great experience and I actually kept that job until I graduated. My books were covered by a scholarship, I was living on campus, the campus buses took students to local stores, I had a full meal plan and the only bill I had was my cell phone bill. Everything was going great, until I discovered I was pregnant on December 5, 2010, just days before finals of my first semester.

Pregnant in College

At this point in time I knew I had to really start budgeting my money if I was going to successfully take care of my child, myself and graduate on time. The next few weeks, not much changed. I set a doctor appointment, I started taking prenatals and I completely focused on my upcoming finals. Before March I had taken on a second job to begin preparing for the arrival of Mr. Sonshine. I saved every dollar I could because I knew babies weren't cheap and I had already confirmed that I would not have access to the family housing options, being that I was not a graduate student. This meant before my son was born I had to move off campus and become a real adult. I would soon become responsible for rent, transportation costs, food, utility bills and the like.

My baby boy was due in August and my goal was to save all the money I could before moving out into the real world. I opted to take on my first loan by applying for summer school. I only took two classes, with the intention of having a reduced schedule my entire sophomore year, three classes each semester. After financial aid, I ended up $5,000 in debt for those six weeks. It gave us time to save and find an apartment, but unfortunately I failed one of the classes. Taking on a complex psych class while nearly eight months pregnant in the dead of summer did not work out for me. I would stay up all night attempting to learn the material and would routinely fall asleep in class. In my defense the professor had a voice reminiscent of the Clear Eyes guy, which did not help at all. I asked for extra credit but I was denied, pregnancy offered me no handicap. Failing the course shook my world because I was now in fear of losing my scholarship, luckily it remained intact. But, I was now motivated more than ever to come back swinging sophomore year, I was determined to not allow my baby to slow me down.

My son's father and I found a low-income apartment about fifteen minutes away from campus when I finished summer school. I was now eight months pregnant and I quickly began to prepare for his arrival. A few of my college friends had helped me throw a baby shower at the end of Spring semester which had given me a leg up on all my essential baby needs such as clothes, bottles, diapers and wipes. I was also surprised with a second shower in the summer by my wonderful co-workers at my work study job. When I look back on this period of my life I am always super appreciative that my employer not only threw me a baby shower that saved me quite a few dollars (primarily on diapers), but they also extended their budget to keep me employed through the summer. I used my savings to buy the final items for my son, such as his scroller and carseat. Now that I was officially off campus and paying rent, I started taking the concept of budgeting a lot more serious. With a household, baby and car to manage, we had to create a monthly plan of action to ensure nothing went wrong.

During this period I made quite a few budgeting, credit and financial mistakes which you will hear about in this book. I started my life as many eighteen year olds do, with no credit and no idea where to start that element of my life. I was taught that credit cards were bad for you and would ruin your credit. Though I was also taught that having no credit was worse than having bad credit. Those two lessons made no sense, they completely conflicted each other. Though there are many ways to build your credit, you typically can't gain access to most of them without having something on your credit. So I did my own research and decided to get a credit card. I was able to use my first two credit cards to start building my credit, which allowed me to buy a brand new car at nineteen and aligned me to buy a house when I was only twenty-four.

I taught myself about finances the same way I learn about all things, through education and experience. I originally educated myself with articles found on NerdWallet.com which gave me a wealth of information on credit cards, banking and loans. I then signed up for CreditKarma.com which gave me information on my credit score, as well as tips on how to increase my score. I started to save money, created a budget every month and started tracking my progress. I started off strong and my credit score was steady growing. But, things quickly became more difficult by the time my son, Deuce, turned two because me and his father had separated and now I was completely on my own managing a household.

It was hard, I won't lie and say that it wasn't but I learned a lot. I graduated on time with my class, I continued to reach my financial goals and my son is proud of me. The fact that you are reading this book lets me know that you may have made some financial mistakes of your own or you just want to increase your knowledge base to successfully prepare your children for a positive financial future. I've been preparing my little guy for a couple years and people are always impressed by his knowledge regarding finance. So, I figured it was time to share, so that you can do the same. Now let's dive in on how you can teach your kids about money, so that they don't make the mistakes that we did.

Where Does Money Come From

The most important lesson that you need to teach your kids about money is where it comes from. If you fail to teach this to your children they will believe that money is endless and stored on your bank card. In this section we will be discussing how to teach your child about where money comes from, how money is earned, as well as the importance of managing money.

Production of Money

If you have a child, I'm sure you've had a conversation with them about how money doesn't grow on trees. But, that typically leaves a lot of confusion for them because they instead begin to think that it grows inside of ATMs. It's important that you clarify that money has limitations and you only have access to the money that you have earned. I taught this to my son by starting from the beginning, how money is printed.

The Federal Reserve is the department that determines how much money will be printed annually. When they believe that the nation needs to increase the money supply they purchase assets. These assets include a range of financial products, primarily government bonds. Bonds are essentially a fixed rate loan from an individual to the government. An individual can buy a fixed rate bond directly from the U.S. Department of the Treasury (home.treasury.gov/services/bonds-and-securities), the term of the bond can range from one year to thirty years. Investors are paid interest on government bonds every six months until it matures. The government uses that additional money borrowed from individuals to fill the gaps in their budget. Once the Federal Reserve determines how much money should be printed that information is then sent over to the Bureau of Engraving and Printing (BEP) who is responsible for the actual printing of bills. Only bills are manufactured at the BEP, all coins are produced by the U.S. Mint bureau.

A great lesson for your kids is to take them on a tour to the closest Federal Reserve bank if possible. There are twelve locations across the country in the following cities: Atlanta, Boston, Chicago, Cleveland, Dallas, Kansas City, Minneapolis, New York, Philadelphia, Richmond, San Francisco and St. Louis. The tour is free and lasts for about an hour. During this tour you and your children will learn about the bank's rules, regulations and payment systems. You also will get to see the actual process of money being counted, sorted and shredded, if you're lucky they will even give your child a bag of shredded money as a souvenir.

After you teach your children about the production of money you can teach them about how it is then put into circulation throughout the economy. The top three questions my son asked me about money were; How did money inside of the ATM? How much money could we take out of the ATM? And what happens to the money that Brinks/Loomis/GardaWorld workers collect? I'm going to give you the answers to these questions in the same manner that I gave them to my son, but always be ready for more questions, children are extremely inquisitive.

Going to the ATM is an exciting adventure when kids first grasp the concept. You pull up to a robot, you stick in your bank card, you enter your top secret password and you are returned with cash. Little people oftentimes think that you can pull out any amount you want, whenever you want. My son once asked for an expensive toy that I did not have on my shopping list, I told him that I did not have the money to buy the item. He looked at me puzzled and suggested that I go and get some more money from the ATM. I laughed, of course, but then explained to him that the money that was in my bank account was for bills, food and savings.

I then showed him a bank receipt and pointed out the withdrawal amount and balance. This gave him a visual of how much money I was able to take out of the ATM. I then taught him that even ATMs could run out of money and that they had to be refilled with money from the bank. Normal sized ATMs can hold up to $200,000, though most only hold $10,000 at a time. When an ATM runs out of money they won't allow any further withdrawals to be taken. A cash loading service is then sent out to refill the machine, this is done by a private courier or an armour carrier. These services load up on cash from local banks and distribute it where it is needed. The most popular companies that we generally see conducting these services are Brinks, Loomis and GardaWorld. These carriers also pickup money from local businesses and take it to the bank for them safely.

Career Choice

Once your child understands where money comes from, talk to your kids about how you earn money. They are a lot more interested in your career than you may think. Many kids are told that "Daddy makes money at work" to a child that may sound like their father actually prints money as his job. Be clear with your children about how income comes in the home. Share with them that money is given to you in exchange for your time, service and labor. Talk to your child about the jobs that the adults in the household go to each day. What do they do at their jobs? How do they get to work? How many hours do they work a day? All of these bits of information will help set realistic expectations in your child's mind about work. In the world of Youtube and eCommerce, many of our youth are under the impression that they can become overnight celebrities. While it's not impossible, it's unlikely. Setting a realistic foundation early when it comes to work will best prepare your child for the future.

If you are an entrepreneur, your answers will be different from the average 9 to 5 worker. Make sure your children are aware of the additional efforts and sacrifices that are required to run your own business. It's not all peaches and sunshine just because you work from home. You can introduce them to a variety of business functions such as marketing, accounting, sales and customer management. In my experience most kids are super interested in the concept of entrepreneurship and typically begin to create their own ideas to build a business of their own.

If you are a stay at home parent talk about your role too. You may not be responsible for bringing in physical money into the home, though the work you do saves the family money. Your stay at home status saves the family childcare costs, in house cleaning services, laundry & dry cleaning services and more. This would be a great time to teach them about bartering. Bartering is the concept of exchanging goods and services with no money involved. For example, your child may offer to unload the dishwasher in exchange for a slice of cake, that's technically bartering. Bartering is actually a great starting point for your child to start learning about money. Though bartering does not involve actual currency, it teaches that nothing is free. Which of course will prove to be true as your child grows older.

Host an in-house career day to teach your kids about the roles of the adults in the home. Make it more interesting by bringing in other family members and friends either virtually or in person. It's great for children to learn early that everyone's role is important and interconnected. While we often highlight the roles of doctors, lawyers and engineers, we realize the importance of janitors, grocery store clerks and the like when cities shut down due to weather or pandemics. Everybody has a role that is vital and necessary, if you remove just one career the entire community could suffer.

Teach your children about how different jobs offer different incomes and the factors that affect pay rate. The top three factors that play into wage setting are education, experience and risk. I love thinking of garbage men when I discuss this topic with little people. They are state workers who make great wages and typically have benefits, but they don't need education or experience to obtain this role. I guess the risk of hanging and jumping off the back of the truck all day makes up for where they lack in the other areas. Teaching about wage factors can assist your child as they grow and determine what type of career they would like to take on.

Education is the primary factor that we are taught that impacts wages. Many of us are encouraged to become doctors and lawyers. Though we are not taught about the huge amount of debt many of us will take on by going that route. Not only will you have to pay back for the actual education, but you will also have to take out loans just to cover your cost of living. Many individuals who are in graduate school don't have the time to work due to the heavy course load, paired with unpaid internships and long study hours. This part of the conversation definitely needs to be discussed with our children before they sign themselves up for a mountain of debt. I attended Emory University on a full ride scholarship and I have quite a few friends who continued their education to become doctors. Many of them regret taking on such a massive amount of debt, resulting in them signing up for loan forgiveness programs. These programs require them to work in low-income communities so that they can have some or all of their student debt forgiven.

Experience is the next wage factor to discuss with your child. The sooner they begin getting work experience, the better. There is a really odd thing thing that happens when young adults are looking for their first jobs. They are required to have two to three years of experience for an entry level job. Of course that makes no sense whatsoever. If this job is the very bottom rung on the ladder, where do you expect that experience to come from? This is probably the reason why over 65% of individuals lie on their resumes. A way to navigate around this is to help your child get a minimum wage job, an internship or hire them yourself. This will ensure that they have some work experience to present to potential employers when they are seeking a job that they actually want.

The final factor that affects wages is risk level or hazardous working conditions. These jobs pay more because there is an increased chance that you can be injured on the job. These roles include but are not limited to construction workers, electricians, taxi drivers, athletes, law enforcement, truck drivers, welders, roofers and pilots. The type and level of danger presented in each of these roles is different. While electricians have to worry about being electrocuted by high voltage wires, taxi drivers have to worry about violent passengers and car accidents. Regardless of what the hazard is, risking your life increases your pay rate. These jobs pay well and are necessary but make sure your children are aware of why these roles pay so well.

I believe that it's important that we don't only encourage our children to become doctors or lawyers, because if they determine that isn't the career for them they will feel as if they failed you. My best friend almost went to medical school because that's what she had told her family that she would do and that's what they expected of her. Luckily after obtaining her Bachelors she decided to follow her calling, which led to a Masters and PhD in a field that she loves.

Choosing a career is one of the most important decisions that your child will make, though they can always change it later, it's always easier if they pursue what they want from the beginning. Introduce them to a range of things and allow them to choose what they like.

My son has been telling me he's going to be a robot engineer since he was five years old. I'm in full support of it, even if that means that he enjoys taking apart old electronics.

Earning Money

Once your child has a grasp of the concept of how money is made, you can teach them how to earn their own money. There are three approaches that parents generally take when it comes to teaching their kids about money. Those three styles are explained below, along with the pros and cons of each.

LEARN & EARN: This approach is one where parents reward their child with money, based on their grades or behavior at school.

Example: An agreement with your child that states. "I will pay you for all of the A's and B's on your report card. For every A, you will receive $10, for every B, you will receive $5. Any grades below a B will not receive any payment at all." You may even compensate for attendance for older children and behavior for younger ones.

- PROS
    - Your child is encouraged to get good grades at school
    - You only have to pay on a quarterly basis

- CONS
    - Some children start to believe that they should always be rewarded for their grades and in the event that they aren't, they will purposely underperform
    - Some children begin to think that they should always be rewarded for doing the right thing

WORK & REWARD: This approach is one where children are paid an allowance or wage for their work. This work can include things like house-chores, completing homework and practicing good hygiene.

Example: Creating a task chart of daily activities that need to be completed. "You need to complete these four tasks everyday Monday through Friday. If they are all completed you will be given $10 at the end of the week. If they are not, you will be paid fifty cents for each task that you did complete."

- PROS
    - You are teaching your child to work for their money, on a daily basis, just like a job
    - Your house is likely to stay cleaner, for a longer period of time
    - You are encouraging consistent responsibility
- CONS

- You typically pay out a lot more with weekly allowance
- Your little person will fuss when their pay is short and you legally can't fire them
- Your child may start to think that they should always receive fiscal compensation for doing the right thing

NO EFFORT ALLOWANCE: This model is one where your child is paid an allowance on the weekly, bi-weekly or monthly basis. This allowance is paid regardless of behavior, chores or grades. It is given on a particular date of the month or day of the week.

Example: An agreement is made with your child to be paid every time you are paid from work. "Every other Friday I will pay you a $10 allowance."

- PROS
  - Your child is continuously earning money and hopefully isn't asking you to buy as many things
  - Your child learns how to manage money based on consistent pay periods
- CONS
  - No work effort is built with this model, the child is not encouraged to perform any better than they did pre-allowance

- Some children may begin to slack off on their normal cleaning and study duties because they know they will receive their allowance regardless

Once your child starts to earn money for themselves they will need to learn how to manage money. Later we will discuss savings and how to teach good saving and investing habits to your children early on, but right now we will just cover the basics. Which option will you select to start teaching your child about money? If your choice is neither, will you allow your child to get a job? How old must they be before you allow them to start working? Will you set requirements on how the money will be spent (i.e. they will be responsible for their own phone bill)? Expectations on spending, saving and household responsibilities should be discussed before your child ever submits an application to reduce future conflict. Another thing that should be discussed is transportation. Many teenagers don't understand or consider the costs associated with getting them to and from work. If the job is not within walking distance, there will be a transportation cost.

Create a game plan with your child about how they will get to and from work. Will you be driving them? If so, how much will they be paying for gas? If you cannot drive them, is there a bus or subway that can take them? If so, what are the costs associated with the bus pass? If they have to use UBER/LYFT does it financially make sense? Many young adults don't consider this cost and end up in a tight spot. For example, if they are making minimum wage at roughly $8 an hour for a six hour shift they are making about $50 before taxes. If the cost to LYFT to work is $15 each direction, that's not a good job for them because they will end up making about $10 a shift. Transportation, taxes and expected hours should all be considered before they agree to take on a job. This will ensure that they don't overwork themselves for little to nothing.

Allowing your child to earn and spend their money independently is a great lesson for financial independence. They start to realize that money has limits when they are faced with wanting something that they cannot afford. They learn to value their money because they have to work hard for it. This typically makes them more appreciative when you spend money on them because they now realize how hard it is to really "make money." It's important that you encourage your children to make responsible choices with their money and not just spend it. Teaching about saving and investing at a young age encourages and prepares your child to have financial success. In the next chapter we will discuss how to manage money so that both you and your children can reach your financial goals.

I always wish that I had started investing sooner. If I had learned to make my money work for me, I would be a lot further in life. But, because it took me years to learn how I almost lost everything after leaving a job. Five months after I bought my house I had to learn some tough lessons on where money comes from. I had been working a corporate job for about two years and I was extremely unhappy. I now had a child and a mortgage, so walking out did not seem like a good idea.

As time went by I became even more unhappy as issues of discrimination occurred and the lack of value for me as a employee became more apparent. One day, I saw an email where my employers were bad mouthing me and my work ethic, I decided that I was over it and I quit. I thought I would be fine being that I had a business of my own and I had eight thousand dollars in savings. I soon learned how difficult it is to make money for yourself without an extremely clear plan of action. Everyday I woke up trying to figure out where my next dollar would come from.

I used LinkedIn to obtain some great clients and I was able to remain self-employed for eighteen months. I ended up making a lot of money with one client in particular but we then had a disagreement due to him not following the contract. Once I released this client I started falling into debt, quickly! My bank account overdrafted when car insurance attempted to pull my monthly payment, I had maxed out my credit cards and I was struggling to make the minimum payments. The credit score that I had worked so hard for, in order to buy my house, began to crash. In an effort to avoid bankruptcy and losing my house, I decided to go back to work. It was a difficult decision to make but I needed a consistent idea of where my money was going to come from.

I was very clear this time around about what I wanted from a job. I wanted to be in a small company, with an employer who valued me and what I brought to the table. I wanted a role that encouraged work-life balance and allowed flexibility, so that I could still have time to be a mom and a business owner. I was able to obtain all of that and more in my current job. I am always grateful for having the opportunity to work for someone who didn't value me, because it really taught me to appreciate when someone did. I now have the best of both worlds with a consistent paycheck and the flexibility to still grow my business and help my clients reach their goals.

What is Money Management?

This question may be one that even adults struggle with. So let's break it down, money pretty much is spent in one of five categories. I know that there are some complex situations that may not fit in either of these categories so feel free to adjust or add a category as necessary. The five categories are bills, saving, investing, fun and debt.

Bills

This is a collective of all expenses that are required for you to live your life in a comfortable, healthy, and independent manner. Some of these items include:

- Rent/mortgage
- Electricity
- Water and sewage
- Food
- Transportation costs
- Internet/cable
- Insurance
- Phone
- Property taxes
- Toiletries
- Childcare

Saving

If you are living financially responsibly, you will have money left after you pay your bills. A good place to put some of this money is in a savings account. Whether you choose to use an account or to store it under your mattress, the goal is the same. You are putting the money away, so that you can access it later. These are a few ways that you can go about saving your money.

- Closeby Cash: This method is when you keep the money extremely closeby, in cash of course. You can store the money, in a sock, safe or someplace else in your home. While this method may be great for people who don't trust banks and who enjoy their money to be in a place that is easily accessible, it is the worst savings option to take. Your money is just sitting there and not working for you at all.
- Savings Account: This method is another option that keeps you funds accessible but you do get a little bit of interest. Though the average bank account typically doesn't pay out more than one percent, it is better than nothing. Online savings accounts are now offering better options that have low minimum requirements with APY (annual percent yield, which is your return on your investment, accounting for compound interest) of nearly 1.35 percent. Bankrate.com is a great tool to shop product options.

- CD's: Certificates of deposit are a wonderful savings tool for people who are serious about reaching their savings goal. This bank product actually puts your money out of reach for a term of 18 months to 5 years. During this time your money is growing interest at a rate of 2 to 2.5 percent.

Investing

How are you making your money work for you? The secret to financial success is not about addition or division, it's about multiplication and subtraction. If you are under the impression that the fastest way to get rich is by saving all your money, piling it to the sky and never sharing, you are wrong. Many of us make this mistake. While we are focused on watching our little pile grow, we are missing out on opportunities that could help it grow into a mountain.

Whether this be an investment opportunity or partnering with someone to collectively reach a larger goal, all of that is missed with the add and divide rule. Investing teaches you to multiply and subtract. You multiply your wealth when you make it work for you, typically through the power of compound interest. In order to make more room in your budget to invest more you must subtract the total of your expense column. What are you paying for that you don't need? What has a low ROI (Return on investment)? Make the cutbacks and adjustments to your budget slowly or increase your income to cover the costs to start investing more.

There are a variety of ways in which you can invest ranging from stocks, to bonds, to real estate, to saving accounts. I suggest that you add a variety of these financial vehicles to your portfolio but only add one at a time. Once you have mastered one investment option then you can build from there. I started investing with Stash which is an app that allows you to buy stocks, partial stocks or entire portfolios based on your investment style. I have since moved to Robinhood which is another extremely user friendly app. I then opened up an IRA account, which is an Individual Retirement Account. Many jobs no longer offer retirement options and packages so it was extremely important for me to get started on this aspect of my future. The next move for me is to enter into the real estate market. I am currently conducting my research on whether I want to buy a property for a long-term tenant or if I want to go the AirBNB/event space route.

Fun

This is where you put all of the extra expenses that don't fall in one of the previous three categories. We all have a spending habit that we can typically remove and still survive. Some examples of these expenses include streaming services, subscription boxes, smoking, drinking, retail of all sorts, books, luxury bath bombs and going out to the club/bar/cigar lounge. This area is usually where people can make the biggest change. I typically put eating out in this category as well, being that it is not a requirement and is so heavily overcharged.

Review your current spending habits and see where you can make the easiest adjustments. Cutting back on this category is usually a first step for people as they seek to decrease their debt to income ratio. When I first started making a change to my financial lifestyle I had to look at my credit card and bank statements to realize where my money was going. Retail and food were my largest categories, with both of them encompassing hundreds of dollars a month.

Debt

I listed this category last because it is the one we hate the most, though it definitely should not be paid last. Your debt is a critical component of building and maintaining your credit score. Your debt includes your mortgage, your car note, your credit cards, your student loans and anything else that has an interest rate on it. If you are interested in becoming debt free, as you should be, then focusing on your debt should be a top priority.

The best method to tackle your debt is to use the snowball method. It is a tactic where you pay off your smallest debt first and then use all funds originally paid to that debt to pay off the next one. I also think it is extremely important to consider the interest rate too when paying off each debt to ensure you are paying the least amount of interest possible. For example if you have two credit cards with the same balance of two hundred and fifty dollars you should pay off the one with the highest interest first. If one has a sixteen percent interest rate and the other has a twenty five percent interest rate, you will pay at least another twenty dollars over the course of a year on the second card in interest. That doesn't seem like a lot but every dollar counts when you are focused on becoming debt free.

Encourage your children not to take on unnecessary debt. Examples of unnecessary debt include car notes, payments for phones, personal loans and excessive student debt. These things can be avoided by paying for these things in cash. Here's some tips regarding these four types of debt:
- If you can wait to get a car, wait. Use the time to save and go buy a car from the auction or local used car dealership. There are many additional fees that are associated with having a car note. Such as interest (of course) and the requirement to pay for full coverage insurance, which you may not have the funds for.
- I have never agreed with paying monthly payments on a phone, it's just not that big of a priority for me. Some people really care about having the newest phone and I believe

that if you need a thousand dollar phone, you should have a thousand dollars in your pocket to make it happen. In many cases you also end up overpaying for the phone, which is why you should always read fine print before agreeing to anything. Every now and then phones are cheaper with this option, but you must be sure there are no additional costs. For example:
- Currently, the newest model of the Apple iPhone is the 11. It can be purchased in full for $999. But, if you purchase the phone through AT&T's payment plan you will end up paying roughly thirty-seven dollars per month for thirty months, a total of $1,110.
- An Apple iPhone SE on the other hand is currently going for $399 in full but only $150 through the same monthly payment program.

- Educational loans are a more acceptable form of debt being that many people only take it on to increase their salary once in the work arena. This additional income would of course be used towards paying off the student debt the first few years following graduation. Whenever possible apply for grant and scholarship opportunities to reduce the overall cost of education. There are scholarships based on gender, race, interests, income and more. There are many databases that house this information such as:
  - https://www.scholarships.com/
  - https://www.naacp.org/naacp-scholarships/

- - https://www.unigo.com/scholarships
  - https://www.salliemae.com/college-planning/college-scholarships/
- Personal loans and payday loans should always be avoided if possible, they typically have extremely high interest rates. I've seen some range up to thirty-three percent!

There are some forms of debt that are easier to maintain and give your credit score a great boost when handled responsibly. One example of this kind of debt includes credit cards, be sure to pay them off in full each month whenever possible. This will give your credit score frequent boosts.

Managing these five categories proves to be extremely difficult for most people. We spend too much. We don't save enough. We don't plan for annual expenses appropriately. Managing money starts with a budget. Discover what you are bringing in and what you are paying out. How much is left? If that value is not enough to meet your goals you'll need to make some changes to ensure that you do reach your goals.

There are three steps to better manage your money. First, review how consistent your spending habits are. If you are going to teach your kids about money, you need to develop some consistent and healthy money habits of your own. If you struggle with compulsive spending or overspending in the fun category, now is the time to make the changes that will change your financial future. Take account of how much you are currently spending and set a goal of how much you would like to be spending instead in each category. Make sure to take time bi-weekly or monthly to review your spending habits.

When I started tracking my spending I realized that I was spending a ridiculous amount of money on food. Once I decided to start eating in the house more and stop eating out as often I was able to cut our food budget in half. This budget cut saved me $3,000 within a year, which allowed me to buy my first house when I was only twenty-four. I teach exactly how to make these cuts to your food budget in my first book, *Saving Money & Time in the Kitchen*.

Next, set goals for the money that sits in the "gap" which is the difference between how much you bring in (income) and how much is paid out (expenses). Where would you like that money to go? To make larger payments toward your debt? To increase your emergency fund? To fund your new business? If you don't have a plan for that money it will more than likely get spent on something that you don't actually need. So set yourself a few goals to avoid blowing your hard earned money. I discuss this in further detail in a later chapter.

Finally, deal with the hard stuff. One of the most important lessons that you can teach your children is to not run from their money problems. Whether you have a debt in collections or a late fee that you want to try and get waived, deal with it. The sooner you make the call and negotiate, the better. If you consistently run from your money issues the more the interest and consequences will build. I once ran from a bill that was in collections, it didn't end well. It resulted in a sheriff serving me to appear in court to discuss my garnishment. At that point I knew I could no longer run from the debt, so I went to the office.

Once there, it was discussed that I could make a payment of whatever amount I wanted and would stay out of the courtroom. I agreed to $200 a month and the super flexible associate listed $100 as my minimum monthly payment. Needless to say a fifteen minute visit allowed me to avoid court and a garnishment of $300 a month. Whenever I can, I make an additional payment towards the principal.

Value of Money

Counting is a critical component in teaching about money and the value of it. Depending on the age of your child, they may already know how to count money. In the event that they do not, remember it's never too early to learn. Start with counting basics. Counting from zero to twenty-five is a great start for money counting. If you are in America, it wouldn't hurt to teach them in Spanish too. Our population is changing and it's best if your child knows simple Spanish so that they can easily communicate with fellow classmates and neighbors.

Teaching your child how to count can prove to be a difficult task in the event that they refuse to focus or aren't interested in talking. I would suggest three things to assisting you with your counting lesson:
1. Count random items (as you clean up toys or wash dishes), often, in the presence of your child,
2. Participate in call and response. Your child can listen to determine if they are saying the number correctly.
3. Don't be aggressive. The worst thing you can do while teaching is to be aggressive. Your child will hate counting if you take this approach.

Introduce them to money and teach them the value of each piece of currency. Once your children are aware of how much each coin and bill is worth then you can begin to teach them about the value of money.

What does value mean? According to the dictionary it means *the regard that something is held to deserve, the importance, worth or usefulness of something.* Many of us miss the mark when teaching our children about the value of money. We spend it carelessly with no regard as to how it will be replenished. Of course we have jobs that we go to everyday and we expect that to be the only source of replenishment that we need, but that couldn't be further from the truth.

As I write this book the current unemployment rate is roughly four percent, which isn't scary to most people. But, this is actually a huge population of people. Last year alone, 21.9 million people were fired or laid off. I had trouble finding data on how many of those people were given severance packages but I can confirm based on knowledge and experience that most of them were given nothing. The COVID19 pandemic has also taught us that many of our jobs are not secure, which is why it is important to have multiple streams of income. What if you got laid off today? Do you have a plan in place on how you would pay your bills and take care of your family? If the answer is no, you may need to start working on a plan of action to value your current income and prepare yourself for the future.

In my home I teach my son that money is earned and therefore should be valued. My work and time is a valuable resource that I can never get back, therefore the pay that I receive in return should be valued as well. How do you value money? By using it to build your future instead of allowing it to vanish the moment it hits your bank account. You should always plan how you will spend your money before it is ever deposited in your account, this will ensure that it won't spend itself. Making a plan will allow you to see if you are living above your means. If you have to use your credit card to buy food or pay bills, you are living above your means and it's time to make some cuts to your expenses.

A simple way to teach your child about the value of money is to convert purchases into hours required to make each purchase. For example, if you get paid $20 an hour and your child is asking for a video game that costs $60, that's three hours of work before taxes. Of course that doesn't sound too crazy to a small person, it's only three hours right? I then suggest that he cleans the house up for three hours straight and then I'll buy him the game. He has never made it past fifteen minutes.

Break it Down

I love to break down my bills to my son in hours, it blows his mind and keeps him from begging me for video games. This is a list of how my hours at work converts to bills, before taxes are deducted.

I suggest that you conduct this activity and share it with your child. To make it more fun and realistic, show your children these values after taxes too.

Mortgage: 46.5 hours
Car Insurance: 14 hours
Electricity: 6.5 hours
Gas Bill: 2 hours
Gas for Car: 6 hours
Water Bill: 3 hours
Internet: 3 hours
Our Phone Bills: 4 hours
Childcare: 12 hours
Food: 17 hours
Debt/Loan Payments: 16 hours
Total Hours: 130 hours

Sidenote: This list doesn't include my business expenses because those are paid for by my business income, which is paid at a different hourly wage.

The average full-time employee works 160 hours a month, so based on my real-life example 81% of my work hours are worked just to pay bills. This means that the remaining 19% is valued and spent wisely. The primary two ways that I value money is by saving and investing. I encourage my son to do the same with his money. Whether he receives money from allowance, as a gift or elsewhere, he is taught to value every dollar. He is still working on long-term savings, but he definitely is grateful for every dollar that makes it to his wallet.

So what should you do with your money once the bills are paid? Invest and save! Think back to the five categories of money management, don't confuse your child by spending more money on the fun category than any other one. If you are frequently buying games/toys, taking them out to the movies/bowling and never saying "no" at the store, they will have trouble understanding that money has limitations. I tell my son "no" sometimes just so that he gets comfortable hearing that word.

Investing

I bring my son in on my investing decisions, not only as a learning experience, but so that he can feel included in building his future. We sit down together and buy stocks as a team. I set an amount of how much we will be investing, then we review and make purchases together. He has learned how to review trends, he reads articles to me aloud about stocks of interest and thus far he has helped me make some pretty good decisions. When children have an understanding of how to make money grow instead of how to make it disappear they are less eager to spend money quickly. Watching stocks rise and fall on the chart is an exciting experience that we share a few times a week.

Saving

Savings on the other hand isn't our strong suit but we're both making progress. We also set saving goals together. Now, I must be honest, saving did not come to me naturally and my son also struggles with this area of finance too. We both have trouble holding on to money that we can easily access. My current goal is to save $500 a month and my son's goal is to save $10. He of course keeps trying to spend his savings on the latest game so I have decided that his savings can NOT be in the home. His savings have to be deposited into his account. Check into your current bank or local credit union to see what your options are for available for your child. Many credit unions allow custodial accounts for children as young as five years old. We'll talk more about this later in the book.

The most important thing about savings is to figure out what method works for you. While I can handle having cash in the home safe, my son cannot and that's okay. I also have learned that I control my impulse to reach into my savings much better when I only have large bills on hand. While pulling out a twenty here and there is convenient and feels harmless, a hundred dollar bill doesn't feel the same. A larger bill makes me really think about the purchase that I want to make and consider if it is even worth it.

The next step in our savings journey is to purchase CD's and bonds, when we finish our research we will be making decisions on how we would like to invest our savings long term. If you are unfamiliar with these two financial products here's a brief summary of what they are and how they can assist you with meeting your savings goals in the long run.

CD: A certificate of deposit is a financial product that operates similar to a savings account. These saving tools offer higher APY rates than a standard savings account, though this money must remain in the account for a certain period of time if you want to receive your deposit and interest back in full. Most CD's require a commitment of six months to five years. If you attempt to withdraw the money early, you will lose money. Most banks and credit unions offer CDs, though the best rates are found with online banking products. While most physical banks require a minimum deposit for $500, online products offered by Ally, Capital One and many other companies don't require a minimum deposit.

Bond: A bond is a loan that you can give to local governments or corporations. Bonds are financial instruments used by these organizations to raise money for particular projects. As a bond holder you are paid interest for holding the bond into the maturity date. If you choose to sell the bond early you may profit being that the worth of a bond can fluctuate like a stock would. You have no ownership in the company with a bond like you do with a stock.

Saving Money & Setting Goals

Saving money is an important step for financial success. The sooner you teach your child about saving, the sooner they can start building their own mini-portfolio. The cool thing about saving is the sooner you start, the higher the payoff is later.

Saving Style

First, decide how your child will save her money. Will it be going into a piggy bank in her room or deposited into her savings account? If it is going in a piggy bank I would suggest that you purchase a digital one that will keep count of how much is put inside. The most common digital money counting jars only count coins and can be found on Amazon or at Walmart for less than fifteen dollars. These banks do not count bills, so if you add a paper dollar you will need to insert a quarter in the slot four times to ensure the count is accurate. Two other options I would suggest would be digital, ATM-like bank that allows your child to use a pin code to gain access (typical price point of twenty dollars and available online) or a complete ATM savings bank that tracks deposits, comes with an ATM card and requires a pin code (available on Amazon for sixty-five dollars).

If you do not choose to purchase a digital bank that will keep up with the deposits, I suggest that you use a Passbook sheet with your child to keep up with the deposits and withdrawals. A Passbook is an extremely old school tool but I do think it is very useful when teaching children about money management, a template is included in the final chapter.

If you choose to save money in the bank, now would be a great time to open your child's first bank account. By separating the money from your account, the money is not only easier to manage but it also gives your child a sense of financial independence. Keep your child updated on the growth of their account and make sure to take them with you when making deposits. If your local bank won't open up an account for your child your credit union typically will.

Next, help your child decide how much money they will be saving from their allowance or any other income. The savings rule can either be a set percentage or a set amount. With Deuce, I encourage him to save twenty percent of whatever he earns or is given. So if he gets one hundred dollars in cash on his birthday, twenty is put into savings. If my grandma gives him five dollars, he's supposed to put one away. A flat rate amount works really good when your child is receiving a consistent allowance. For example, they earn fifteen dollars a week and they save five dollars each week. It's all about what works best for the both of you. Don't get irritated if you receive some push back, most kids like to spend way more than they like to save. My son only saves up to sixty dollars, at that point he can buy a new game for his Switch. I used to protest with him about it, but now I just let him do what he wants. He is consistently saving for a goal, so at least he is progressing in that area.

Third, make decisions on what they are saving for. Is it a small, short-term goal like a game or playset? Or is it something long-term, like a car? As I said in the last paragraph my son likes to save for video games, maybe your child does the same or maybe they want to save for something more substantial like college. I've also seen young children save for their business ideas. For example, if a child wants to start a lawn care service they may set a goal of saving two hundred dollars to buy a used mower and weed wacker to get started.

The final part of this planning would be to estimate how long it will take to reach the goal based on the savings strategy that you two developed. Let's use our lawn care example again, with a goal of two hundred dollars. Your child receives an allowance of ten dollars a week and they have decided to put half of that allowance into their savings. So at a rate of five dollars a week it would take forty weeks or roughly ten months for your child to reach their goal. If that timeline doesn't work for them and they would like to meet their goal sooner they would either need to find more money or adjust their savings strategy.

Money doesn't grow on trees, so unless they decide to crowdfund with their aunts and uncles, a strategy adjustment may be easier. Maybe they will instead save five dollars a week on even weeks and eight dollars on odd weeks. This will allow them to reach their goal in thirty-one weeks which is a little less than eight months. Cutting their timeline may put them in position to start cutting grass at the beginning of the summer instead of at the end of the summer. Their sacrifice will payoff, as an increase in profit to their newfound business.

In order to keep your child motivated and encouraged on their new savings journey, make a visual! I have created a sample goal sheet that you can copy and have your child shade in as they complete each milestone. You can find this graphic in the final chapter of this book. Consistency and encouragement will keep your child focused on reaching their goals.

You too should be saving money for your child's future. Most people like to save for their child's college fund or for their first car. I'm not exactly for or against college, so while I don't shove it down my son's throat that I want him to go, I also don't discourage him from taking that route if he feels it is necessary. Being that this is my stance my son doesn't have a "college fund." I instead have a "Financially Focused Future" account for him. This money can be used to pay for college, fund his first business or to buy his first property. I am open to whatever he would like to do with the money, though I need him to write up a plan of action and be at least seventeen before it is released to him.

529 Plans

If you are interested in saving for your child's future college education I encourage you to look into a 529 College Savings Plan. This financial tool allows you to save for college, graduate school or for K-12 tuition, tax-free. There are thirty-five states that actually give income tax deductions or tax credits. Each state offers a variety of plans, so shop around for the one that best fits your needs and gives you the lowest fees. Savingforcollege.com has an interactive map that lists all the options for each state, you can access it here: www.savingforcollege.com/529_plan_details/ Some states also assist by giving a contribution for plans opened for infants or match the contributions of low-income parents.

Another benefit of 529 plans is that there are no mandatory monthly payments required, payments can be as little as twenty-five dollars and anybody can make payments towards the account. Individuals can contribute up to $15,000 a year before they are responsible for gift taxes. As the owner of the account you can choose how you would like the money to be invested based on your risk tolerance. There are a range of ways in which the money can be invested including, stocks (both domestically and internationally), bonds, real estate funds and CD's.

In the event that your child chooses not to go to college you have three options for the funds. You can transfer the funds to an eligible child such as a sibling, cousin, niece, nephew, aunt or uncle of the beneficiary. You can use the funds in the future for an eligible family member such as a grandchild, a child, niece or nephew of the original beneficiary. Or the funds can be withdrawn, though taxes and penalty fees will apply to the earned portion of the funds.

There is another program that many parents have taken advantage of, prepaid tuition plans, these are also considered to be 529 Plans. They were set up to allow you to lock in today's tuition prices for the future. Unfortunately, college tuition prices are rapidly increasing and the investment returns don't meet the mark. Which means these plans are starting to fade away as individuals lose trust in this plan being that they don't offer any guarantees.

Coverdell Education Savings Accounts (ESA) are another option for planning for college expenses. ESA options have more restrictions than most 529 plans, the main one is that only $2,000 can be contributed to the account annually. The second drawback is that no deposits can be made after the child is eighteen. Reasonable speaking most people would be reaching in to pull money from the account at that age. But, if your child received a full-ride to undergrad you could hold on to the money and continue to grow it in a normal 529 plan, until they reached graduate school. A benefit of the Coverdell account is that you could use the funds for elementary and secondary school expenses and not just tuition like a 529 plan.

Outside of education expenses, the next biggest expense for your child is typically a car. Owning a car will give your child a sense of independence and will reduce some errand running for you. This decision should be carefully considered to ensure it is most beneficial for you and your child. A teenager does not need a new car, nor do they need an expensive car. These two factors will only increase your insurance premium (be sure to sign your child up for a defensive drivers course to receive an additional discount), but will also increase your maintenance costs and car note payments. Stick to buying an affordable used car that your child can afford to put gas in and get fixed if an issue pops up. I also recommend that you have your child match you or at least put something towards the cost of the vehicle. It is human nature to take better care of things you paid for yourself.

Buying a Car

There are a variety of ways that you can go about purchasing a used car. You can attend a local auction or dealership. You can use social media to access local deals from individuals and dealers. You can reach out to family and friends to see who is ready to part with their old vehicle. Whenever possible get a Carfax report and have a mechanic check out the car PRIOR to purchase. I learned my lesson about this the hard way when I bought my first car at the age of eighteen.

I needed a car to get to work, school and to drop my son off at daycare. So, I found a car on Craigslist for $2,200 and went and paid for it cash after test driving it. This turned out to be one of the biggest mistakes of my life. After two weeks I had trouble turning my wheel, thank goodness I didn't get into an accident. Though I had bought the car AS IS I was able to convince the seller to fix the issues. Six weeks after the date of purchase my engine blew out on the freeway on my way to class. Turns out there was a crack in my engine that likely would have been found if I had a mechanic look at the car, but it definitely was exacerbated by me not getting an oil change. I was attempting to do everything on my own, though I definitely should have seeked out a professional for this purchase. I was able to junk the car for $300 cash and was back at square one.

When it comes to saving money and setting goals, your child needs your help. These are both very new tasks for them but with your guidance they can be successful and make fewer mistakes than we did. Though young people aren't the best money managers, this is typically due to lack of knowledge. If you instill financial knowledge in their lives while they are young they will be more competent and capable.

Take the Fear out of Finance

The number one mistake that parents make when teaching their kids about money (if they teach them anything at all) is passing on the lesson of fear. Money can be a scary topic. With the fears ranging from bankruptcy to divorce. But, this is something that is taught. If you encourage your children to feel empowered by their finances at an early age, that lesson will stick with them for life. So how do you teach your kid to be empowered by something that may be a scary subject for you? You get out of your fear and you show them with your actions that you can control your finances and direct them towards success.

Being a Good Example

First, deal with your finances head on. Know how much income you are bringing in and how much you are paying out in expenses. Know how much debt you have. Once you are aware of your finances you can make a game plan on how to get ahead, pay off your debt, invest and retire early.

Next, put the plan to work and bring your kiddo(s) in the loop. Explain to them where debt comes from and how interest works against you. Instead of telling them "we can't afford that" explain to them that you have money, but it is going to be spent on priorities and not that $97 Lego set. Breakdown the budget for them. You don't have to go line item by line item on your budget, but give them understanding of the true cost of living. My son loves to tell me that I have money and that I have $2,000 in the safe whenever I deny purchasing him a game or toy. The last time he made this statement I laughed at him and quickly broke down at least $3,000 of monthly bills. Needless to say he now understands that that money is for emergencies and truly isn't that much if an actual emergency was ever to occur.

Finally, teach them the right way by exhibiting your mistakes. Being that I was a huge emotional spender when I was younger, it is very important to me that I teach my son to set saving goals. Most times he sets goals, reaches them and spends the money on that big ticket item he was eyeing that I refused to buy for him. He is learning to be responsible and not to impulsively spend because that will slow him down from his goal. Whatever your biggest financial mistake was, ensure that it becomes your child's most important lesson instead of their biggest fear.

Financial Activities

A positive money mindset is key to a successful financial future. Make sure that your children feel confident with their money. The best way to build this confidence is to promote and teach financial literacy. Here are a few activities to dive your child into the world of financial literacy:

- Take them to the bank with you. As technology continues to get better and better, the brick and mortar world is quickly slipping away from us. Take advantage of these learning opportunities while they are still available before we move to a completely digital world. Show them how to fill out deposit and withdrawal slips.
- Introduce them to the stock market. There are tons of easy apps that you can download to show them, if you don't have them already. I personally use and enjoy Robinhood, Stash is also a good option. I have taught my son how to review a stock's recent performance, determine if a stock is a "good" buy and review our returns.
- Count money together. You can open up the piggy bank and roll coins or pull the money out the safe and count how close you are to your savings goal.
- Take them grocery shopping with you. When I prepare my grocery list I estimate a price for each item and a total for the trip. My son usually holds the list and pen or my phone if we are using a digital list. He marks things off as we go and points out when an item is over budget. I was so proud when he suggested that I put back the cut cantaloupe and get the sliced cantaloupe instead because it would save us two dollars.
- Take them with you when you are making a big purchase such as a car or a house. As you are reviewing each option discuss the pros and cons with your child, such as the price,

the features, the age and the amenities. My son actually picked out our house. We had been looking at houses for two weeks for two or three days each week. When we entered our house there were so many things I loved about it and that met my must-have list. My only complaint was that the house didn't have a two car garage. I guess my lack of complaining was a green light for him because he walked over to the grill that came with the house and snatched off the bow. I asked him why he had done that and my then five year old proudly said, "it's our grill because it's our house." Turns out, he was right.

- Play money themed board games with them such as: Monopoly, Life, In Home Banking or Payday.
- Let them attend your weekly or monthly financial meeting. If you are the only adult in the house and typically conduct your review independently, change that. Talk about upcoming bills and incoming deposits. If there are holidays, maintenance fees or trips coming up discuss how you will financially prepare for the additional expenses.

I also encourage you to get started with building your child's credit while they are still minors. This is a great lesson for both of you and it is an easy way for them to see something tangible from all of your financial strategies. Nothing will better prepare your child for financial success than a healthy credit score. Many parents aren't aware of how they can start building their child's credit so I'm going to share a couple tips with you to get started.

Building Your Child's Credit

The first strategy is to add your child as an authorized user to your credit card. Many banks don't have a minimum age requirement for authorized users, so that means children as young as five can be added to your card without an issue. When they get older and more responsible you can give them their card. Be sure to check with your credit company and see if they offer the ability to place limits on the authorized user's spending. Before you add your child to your credit card be sure that your card is in good standing and ensure you are using your card to build your credit effectively. It does them no good to be added to a card in bad standing. I used my credit cards as the primary tool to increase my credit score by nearly one hundred points in less than seven months before I bought my house. Here's my top tips to use your credit card to increase your credit score:

- Ensure you are getting the best interest rate possible. In my personal opinion you should be aiming for something at or below twenty percent, which is not always possible for your first card but it is a good goal. Make this easy for yourself by shopping around for the best offer by using creditcards.com. They offer a card matching tool that gives you access to a range of products that you should qualify for based on your credit score. This site does not put a hard inquiry on your credit. Many people I know choose CapitalOne as their first card, they have a few great cards. Also, note that when you are being a great cardholder you will be given an increase in credit and you can even request a lower interest rate.

- Do not over utilize your card! I suggest that you never use more than thirty percent of your credit limit. If you have a credit limit of three hundred dollars, don't use more than ninety dollars and when possible pay it in full every month. Also, be sure to not underutilize your card. If you have a card that you do not use, it does nothing at all for your credit.
- Pay your credit card bill twice a month. First, make sure you are paying more than the minimum payment whenever you can. This will ensure that you pay the least amount of interest possible. When you pay twice a month you end up making at least thirteen payments a year instead of twelve. You will see a consistent increase in your credit score. Your score updates every seven days on Credit Karma, therefore twice a month your card will be reporting a new payment and hopefully a lower balance.

A second strategy to start building your minor's credit is to list them on a car loan. In the previous chapter I discussed the benefits of buying a used car in cash, though if you decide to sign up for a car note you might as well allow your child to benefit from it. While some lenders will not allow a minor to be the lead on the loan, others won't allow them to be the co-signer. So be sure to do your research and see what options are available from your bank, credit union and the car dealership. Be sure to pay the note on time, pay extra to the principal when possible and split the payment in half and pay twice a month before it is due for maximum increase to your credit.

Parts of a Credit Score

Be sure to teach your child about the components that determine your credit score. There are six factors that make up your credit score:

1. Payment History: This is probably the most important factor of your credit. It is based on if you are paying your bills on time. Pay all your bills on time and early when you can and your credit will flourish.
2. Credit Usage: This is another heavy weighing factor on your credit, as I discussed previously in this book, you should try to utilize less than thirty percent of your credit limit. The closer you are to the limit, the worse this weighs in on your credit.
3. Derogatory Marks: This category is typically where collections and missed payments are listed. If you have a

repossession or foreclosure it will be in this category too. It is important that you get whatever you can out of collections and work diligently to make your payments on time to offset any missed payments.

4. Length of Credit History: This factor of your credit is one that you can't do much to fix. All you can do is be patient. One thing I would recommend is to never close your old (particularly your oldest) accounts. If you opened your first credit card five years ago, your credit report will be five years old. If you close that account your credit age will reduce back to your next oldest account, which may only be three years old. Even if you pay off a card completely don't close it, use it for gas or something small and pay it in full before the due date each month to best improve your credit.

5. Credit Inquiries: Any time your credit is pulled, you receive an inquiry. There are two types of inquiries, soft and hard. While soft inquiries do not affect your credit at all, hard inquiries usually lower your credit by a few points until they fall off. It generally takes two years for an inquiry to fall off of your report. Keep this in mind when you are getting your credit pulled multiple times to buy a car, request a loan or obtain a credit card.

6. Mix of Accounts: There are two types of credit accounts that can be applied to your credit, installment accounts and revolving accounts. Installment accounts are items that have a balance that doesn't increase, that you are paying

off in monthly payments. Examples include car notes, loans and mortgages. Revolving accounts are items that fluctuate in value such as credit cards. It is best that you have some of both of these accounts on your credit.

I grew up in a household where money was scarce and I was very afraid of what my financial future held in store. My grandmother took great care of me, I never went hungry, our lights were never cut off and I always had clean clothes. Though, I knew that we didn't have much left for anything extra, even if it was just money to go to the movies. I was afraid that I would grow up and have limited funds too. I wanted to buy a house and car and have a business of my own, but I always thought that I was being unrealistic. When I went off for college I landed a job within my first week on campus. My only bill was my phone bill and being that I didn't have any knowledge on how to manage money, I generally blew the rest on clothes, shoes and fun.

I didn't learn how to manage money until five months later when I discovered I was pregnant. I began to save nearly every dollar I made in preparation for his arrival. By giving your child the gift of financial literacy they will learn that they can have their cake and eat it to. They will be able to enjoy their young lives, while still preparing for their future.

Banking for Kids

Bank Accounts

Many credit unions, as well as some of the big branch banks have saving programs and accounts for children. There are quite a few options available depending on your financial institution so ensure that you check with them first to gain more details on the programs you and your child qualify for.

Most banks have their program options listed based on the age of the child. While options for small children don't typically offer any benefits, mid-age children (typically seven or older) are most times offered additional information about finances presented either by mail or through email marketing. Pre-teens and teenagers are typically given access to checking accounts too. These accounts are joint accounts of their parents, though still give them a sense of responsibility when they are presented with a debit card that has their name on it.

Investing

Stocks are another option that are available for your children as young as two years old (maybe younger). To get started quickly and affordably Stash is a great option. Signing up is quick and easy on stashinvest.com and you only need five dollars to get started. In order to maximize your investments it's best to start early. Wouldn't you have loved it if your parents started your investment portfolio for you?

I have a few friends who had great credit scores when we were only nineteen years old. I decided to ask more questions and I discovered that their parents had gotten the ball rolling for them. Whether it was listing them as a co-signer on a car or as a designated user on a credit card, the results were the same. Having credit at an early age is a blessing and a curse. The only way to avoid the curse, is by being knowledgeable about credit and finances. Being that you are reading this book, I know that you plan on teaching these things to your child to help them avoid that difficult lesson.

Many people are interested in investing for their child but they are unsure about how custodial accounts work. Custodial accounts are controlled by the adult party on behalf of a minor. When your child comes of age (either 18 or 21 depending on your state) the account is transferred to them and you lose all control of the account. There are many benefits of setting your child up a custodial account, one benefit is the reduced tax rate. Minors who are filed on your taxes are allowed a certain amount of unearned income to be accessed at a reduced tax rate.

There are many financial institutions that offer custodial investment accounts including: TD Ameritrade, Charles Schwab, Ally Bank, Vanguard, Stockpile, Etrade and Fidelity. I also just discovered a platform called Loved (loved.com), which I have signed up for. This platform has great reviews and supposedly is completely commission free, I'm hoping we have a great experience with this platform as I plan for Deuce's future. When shopping around for the best custodial account for your needs be sure to check out what options each institution has and be sure to read the fine print. The primary options that you will see are:

- UTMA/UGMA (Uniform Transfers to Minors Act/Universal Gifts to Minors Act): These are the acts that regulate custodial accounts in the United States but they are often used as a synonym for custodial investment accounts.
- Roth/Traditional IRA: Both of these are great options when really thinking long-term for your child and their eventual retirement. A Roth IRA is a bit better because it is more flexible when it comes to withdrawing money from the account. There are a variety of penalty free ways to withdraw money early such as to buy a first home or to cover expenses due to a disability.
- Savings Accounts: These accounts are pretty similar to normal savings accounts, they have fixed interest rates and don't grow as quickly as other investment vehicles would.

The fine print is important primarily when it comes to withdrawing from the account. Some accounts have restrictions on when the money can be taken while others are focused on what the money is being spent on. Make sure that the fine print matches your financial goals for your child to avoid unnecessary penalties. Also, be sure to check into the maximum contributions allowed for the account, ensure that it also aligns with how much you plan on depositing on behalf of your child.

Kidpreneurs

This generation of kids are probably the smartest, most tech-savvy set of kids we've ever seen. These kids pop out the womb knowing how to work a smart phone. My son comes up with business ideas all the time and his friends do too. If your child is a mini-entrepreneur I encourage you to support their dreams. Use their bank accounts when they first get started, until they are required to register their business, at which point they should get a business bank account. In most states a business license or at least an operating permit is required once the "business" grosses more than four hundred dollars. I work with clients at The Sonshine Enterprise file their business licenses everyday, so just reach out if you need help with incorporation. Based on my knowledge no state allows a child to be the organizer listed on a business license. So the business license and account will have to be registered in your (or some other adult's name) until they are of age. This trusted individual will be responsible for executing contracts on behalf of the business and will manage all funds until the child is old enough and competent enough to handle these tasks independently.

There are so many lessons that your child can learn about money by running their own business. Product based businesses and service based businesses are a little different when it comes to overhead but most of the lessons are the same.

- EXPENSES/OVERHEAD: Whether your child is running a lemonade stand or cutting lawns, they will soon discover that running a business costs money. Examples:
    - Product-based business: A lemonade stand requires lemons, cups, sugar, ice, pitcher, straws and possibly a marketing budget for a sign and flyers.
    - Service-based business: A mini-landscaper would have to pay for initial equipment such as a lawn-mower and a weed-eater. They would also need to pay for items to maintain each yard such as leaf bags, gasoline and trimmer line.
    - These costs will help your young entrepreneur determine how to set their costs to ensure they make a profit.
- MARKETING: How will you attract customers? There are a variety of ways to gain customers and each business is

different when it comes to marketing. Some examples of marketing include:
- Word of mouth, a happy customer will always send more customers your way.
- Flyers, hang them in places where your ideal customer is likely to see them.
- Social media, a great tool to share your products and services and keep your clients updated with what you have planned next.
- Email/text marketing, developing an email/phone list of current and potential clients is a great resource for future sales. Whenever you release something new, have a special offer or just would like to check in, you can send an email/text to your entire list in one shot.

- SALES & PROFIT: These are two terms that kids easily mix up, though as entrepreneurs they will quickly learn the difference. While a sale is the amount of money made during a transaction, profit is the money that the business owner actually gets to keep after paying for expenses. Business also teaches your child about one-time sales and recurring sales. Some clients will be consistent and committed while others are just one-offs.
- CUSTOMER SERVICE: This is one of the most important lessons that could ever be taught in business. Customer service is all about how you treat people. Did you greet them with a smile? Did you say thank you after their

purchase? Did you assist them with their issue without getting an attitude? These skills are not only important as a business owner, but as a customer and as an overall good citizen. The earlier your child learns this skillset, the better off they'll be.

- PROBLEM SOLVING: No matter what type of business you go into, problems will arise. Having the ability to solve those problems are great opportunities for both you and your children to think outside the box. It can be something as simple as figuring out how to stop the cups from blowing off the lemonade stand or as complex as figuring out the best spot in the neighborhood to set up the stand to gain the most customers.

Why Does This Matter?

The world is changing and if you don't plan for these changes your family won't survive. A big change that is rapidly happening is the advancement of technology. Manual labor skills will no longer take you as far as they did thirty years ago. Which means we all have to get comfortable with coding, operating in a world of digital marketing and artificial intelligence. Without these skills it will be extremely difficult to make a living. Even with these skills it may be difficult to make a living because there will be more and more robots filling the positions. Our parents grew up in a time where you didn't need a lot of education to secure a decent job. They could work at a factory, warehouse or steelyard for thirty years and retire happily and comfortably. That is not an option for us or our children. The cost of living is ever increasing and salaries are not keeping up. The best way to prepare yourself for success is to make your money work for you.

Make sure your children are not creating debt that they don't need, we talked about this in a previous chapter but I want to focus on it regarding education. The price of higher education is one of the most expensive forms of debt a person can take on, outside of buying a house. The unfortunate part about investing in higher education is that the payoff isn't there like it used to be. Many huge employers such as Google, IBM, Apple and Bank of America have decided to drop their college degree requirement for new recruits.

This means they are solely focused on the experience and skills that a candidate brings to the table. In June 2020, an Executive Order was passed requiring federal jobs to be filled with individuals with the required skills, no longer relying or requiring college experience. Instead of investing thousands of dollars into an education, you can instead help your child find a paid or unpaid internship that can help them build skills for success.

The payout in salary based on education has an extremely large gap for the Black community, particular women. One study conducted by the AAUW (American Association of University Women) shows that the median white adult who dropped out of high school, has seventy percent more wealth than the median black adult with a college degree. When you review the data compiled by The LeanIn Organization you will discover that the gap widens between Black women and all men as education increases. When both have less than a high school diploma, the gap is a twenty-three percent difference. Once both have a college degree or higher, the gap increases to thirty-five percent!

Education doesn't close the wealth or pay gap. When you disregard education and compare Black women to white men, you will see that the women only make sixty-two cents for every dollar earned by the men. This is extremely alarming when you consider the fact that eighty percent of Black mothers are the sole providers of their households. If Black women were paid fairly they would make an average of $950,000 more throughout their career. To me, this means two things, we need to do something about the wage gap and we need to stop giving our kids a four year delayed start and a pile of debt, while others are helping their kids start business straight out of high school.

I have shared a lot of information on how to get started with your child's investment portfolio but there is another way that you can give your children a financial advantage, residual income. Residual income comes when you put in the work on something once and then you reap the benefits for years to come. Examples of this include writing books or producing music. Once the book is written or the album is released, outside of marketing, no other work is required to make money off of the product. If you list your child as a co-author of your book (such as I did) or as the executive producer of your album (such as Nas did on Stillmatic) your child can forever profit off of the sales and royalties. Think about what products you can create that can create a source of income for your children forever.

Financial Terms

The earlier your child is exposed to financial terms, the better. You want to set them up for a successful future built off of strategic investments and multiple streams of income. My son is only eight years old and has independently come up with four profitable business ideas. I'm not sure if he has it naturally or because of his knowledge base regarding business and finances. The following list contains the first twenty-two financial terms that I taught my son. The definitions are written in a simplistic fashion to help you child best catch on. I created matching flashcards based on how my son describes each term. The list below has a more thorough definition of each term for your own knowledge or in case your child has follow-up questions regarding the terms.

Another lesson that I want to get across before I wrap up this book is to never be afraid to learn with your kids. I know that there is this weird expectation that parents are supposed to know everything, but that's just not reality. Whenever my son (or my nephew) asks me about something that I don't know the answer to I never say "I don't know." Instead I say "I'm not sure, let's find out." We then go on a journey together to find out why blueberries are blue or how does a remote connect to a TV. Knowledge does not have limitations, there is always more to learn. I hope that this book encourages you and your children to want to learn and discover more about money, finances, investments and the world ahead of us.

1. **ASSET:** Something or someone who makes you money, such as equipment for your business or an amazing employee
2. **BOND:** A loan that you can give to local governments or corporations. These financial instruments are used by these organizations to raise money for particular projects
3. **BUDGET:** A financial tool that helps you manage your money by determining how it will be spent
4. **CREDIT CARD:** A financial tool that allows you to spend money that you don't have, you will be responsible for making a small payment of what you owe every month. You will be charged interest if you do not pay the money back in full before the monthly due date
5. **CREDIT LINE:** The amount of money that you have been loaned from a financial institution and can spend, though it must be paid back. Credit cards are the most common type of credit lines, though you can also get a business or personal credit line from a loan provider
6. **CREDIT SCORE:** A number that expresses your creditworthiness based off of your credit performance. A score below a 620 is considered bad credit, a 850 is a perfect score

7. **CURRENCY:** Money in any form that is circulated through the economy usually in the form of coins and bills. Every country uses their own form of currency
8. **DEBIT CARD:** A card that is linked to your checking account, when you make purchases they are deducted from that account immediately. Debit is the equivalent to cash, no fees involved when making purchases. You can also use this card at an ATM to take money directly out of your account, you may have to pay a fee when you don't go to your bank's ATM
9. **DEBT:** Amount of money owed to a financial institution or a person, money that has been borrowed and promised to be paid back
10. **DIRECT DEPOSIT:** Money sent directly into your bank account through an electronic transfer, typically an option for your check from your employer
11. **EMERGENCY FUND:** Money that you save to prepare for emergency situations such as your car breaking down or you getting sick and missing work
12. **GROUP ECONOMICS:** Individuals putting their money together to collectively invest in something that they could not have purchased independently
13. **INTEREST:** Fee you are charged for borrowing money from a financial institution. Interest is charged to mortgages, credit cards and personal loans, generally at a flat rate

percentage of the amount owed, paid in increments monthly with the principal

14. **INVESTMENT:** To put your money into something with the expectation of a financial return in excess of the original amount you put in
15. **INVESTOR:** An individual that puts their money into a financial vehicle in an effort to make more money
16. **LIABILITY:** Something or someone that costs you time or money
17. **NEPOTISM:** When a person uses their power to help their family and friends, typically by providing them with jobs
18. **PRINCIPAL:** The original amount of money borrowed on a loan or a put into an investment
19. **ROI:** Return on Investment, how much you gain on a particular investment
20. **STOCK:** To own a small piece of a company, when that company profits you do too, when the company loses money, the value of your stock goes down
21. **TAXES:** Money that you have to pay to the government when you earn money and when you spend money
22. **WAGES:** Value that you are paid for a particular period of time to complete work

Savings Chart

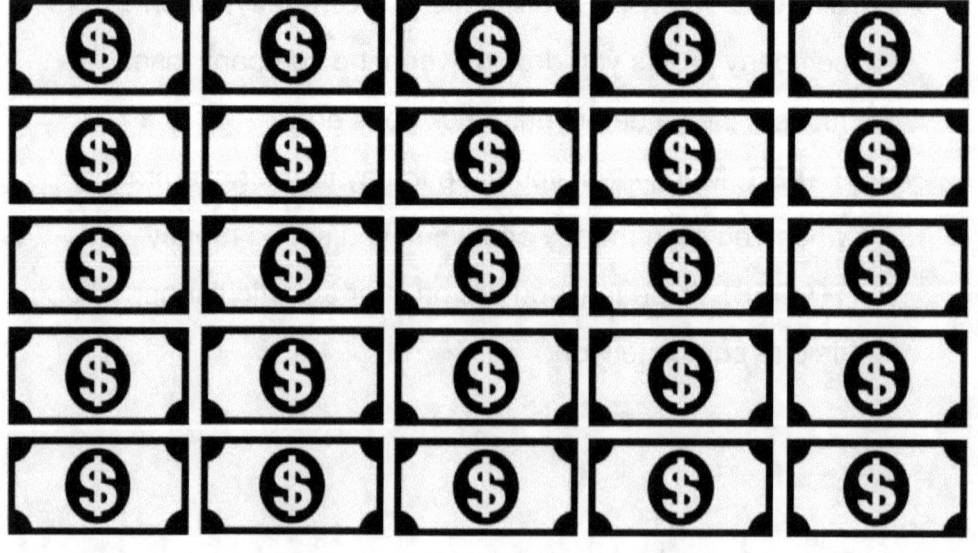

$5 $10 $15 $20 $25

Goal Worksheet

EARNINGS

How much would you like to make per week? _____

How much do you make per week? _____

What is the difference? _____

What are some ways that you can increase your income? _____

_____

SAVINGS

What are you saving for? _____

How much does it cost? _____

How much will you save per week? _____

How long will it take you to reach your goal? _____

INVESTING

How much would you like to invest per week? _____

Where will you be investing this money? _____

What is your investing goal for the year? _____

What is the average return for the investment you have in mind?

_____

ANNUAL FINANCIAL GOALS

_____

_____

_____

Savings Passbook

DATE	WITHDRAWALS	DEPOSITS	BALANCE

Flashcards

ASSET

BOND

Flashcards

Something or someone who makes you money or saves you time

A loan that you can give to local governments or corporations to fund particular projects.

Flashcards

BUDGET

CREDIT CARD

Flashcards

A financial tool that helps you manage your money by determining how it will be spent

---

A financial tool that allows you to spend money that you don't have, you will be responsible for making a small payment of what you owe every month

Flashcards

CREDIT LINE

CREDIT SCORE

Flashcards

The amount of money that you have been loaned from a financial institution and can spend, though it must be paid back

A number that expresses your creditworthiness based off of your credit performance

Flashcards

CURRENCY

DEBIT CARD

Money in any form that is circulated through the economy usually in the form of coins and bills

A card that is linked to your checking account, when you make purchases they are deducted from that account immediately. Debit is the equivalent to cash

Flashcards

DEBT

DIRECT DEPOSIT

Flashcards

Amount of money owed to a financial institution or a person, money that has been borrowed and promised to be paid back

---

Money sent directly into your bank account through an electronic transfer, typically an option for your check from your employer

---

Flashcards

EMERGENCY FUND

GROUP ECONOMICS

Flashcards

Money that you save to prepare for emergency situations such as your car breaking down or you getting sick and missing work

Individuals putting their money together to collectively invest in something that they could not have purchased independently

Flashcards

INTEREST

INVESTMENT

> Fee you are charged for borrowing money from a financial institution. Interest is charged to mortgages, credit cards and personal loans

> To put your money into something with the expectation of a financial return in excess of the original amount you put in

Flashcards

INVESTOR

LIABILITY

Flashcards

An individual that puts their money into a financial vehicle in an effort to make more money

Something or someone that costs you time or money

Flashcards

NEPOTISM

PRINCIPAL

Flashcards

When a person uses their power to help their family and friends, typically by providing them with jobs

The original amount of money borrowed on a loan or a put into an investment

Flashcards

ROI

STOCK

Flashcards

Return on Investment, how much you gain on a particular investment

To own a small piece of a company, when that company profits you do too, when the company loses money, the value of your stock goes down

Flashcards

TAXES

WAGES

Flashcards

Money that you have to pay to the government when you earn money and when you spend money

Value that you are paid for a particular period of time to complete work

www.ingramcontent.com/pod-product-compliance
Lightning Source LLC
LaVergne TN
LVHW051507070426
835507LV00022B/2975